mommy

mamma

daddy

papà

boy

bambino

girl

bambina

1 **one**

uno

2 **two**

due

3 **three**

tre

4 **four**

quattro

5

five

cinque

6

six

sei

7

seven

sette

8

eight

otto

9

nine

nove

10

ten

dieci

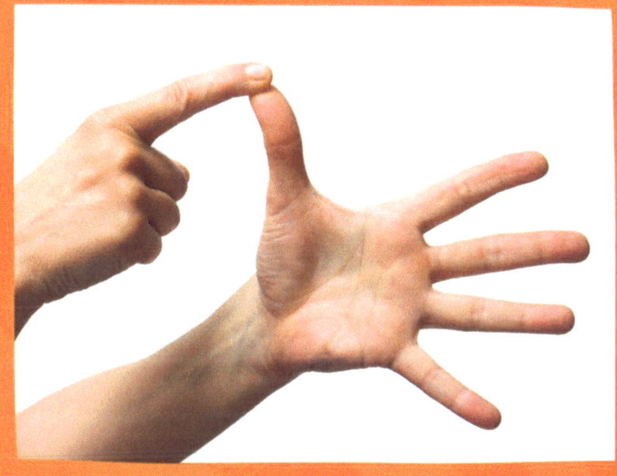

count

contare

write

scrivere

draw

disegnare

paint

dipingere

circle

cerchio

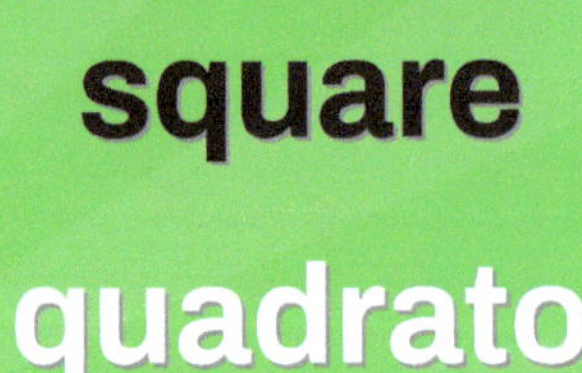

square

quadrato

rectangle

rettangolo

triangle

triangolo

star

stella

black

nero

white

bianco

brown

marrone

red

rosso

blue

blu

yellow

giallo

green

verde

purple

viola

gray

grigio

orange

arancione

pink

rosa

apple

mela

banana

banana

pineapple

ananas

watermelon

cocomero

pear

pera

grapes

uva

mango

mango

peach

pesca

strawberry

fragola

cherry

ciliegia

orange

arancia

coconut

cocco

lemon

limone

mushroom

fungo

corn

mais

tomato

pomodoro

pumpkin

zucca

cucumber

cetriolo

carrot

carota

potato

patata

zucchini

zucchina

spinach

spinacio

cauliflower

cavolfiore

egg

uovo

plate

piatto

spoon

cucchiaio

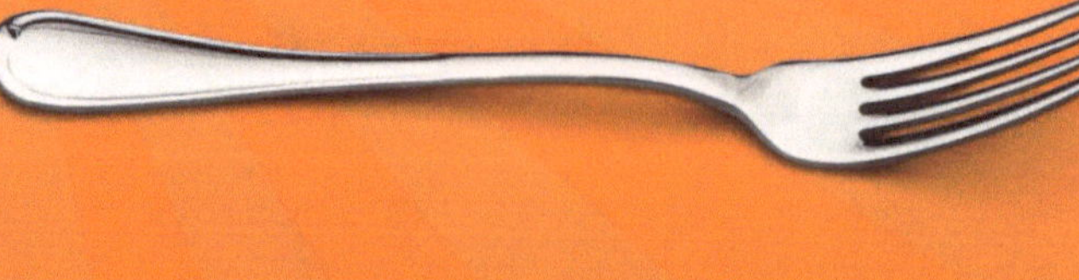

knife

coltello

fork

forchetta

cake

torta

baby bottle

biberon

candies

caramelle

cheese

formaggio

drink

bere

eat

mangiare

hot

caldo

cold

freddo

small

piccolo

big

grande

 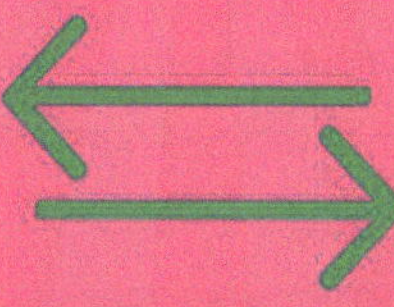

short

corto

long

lungo

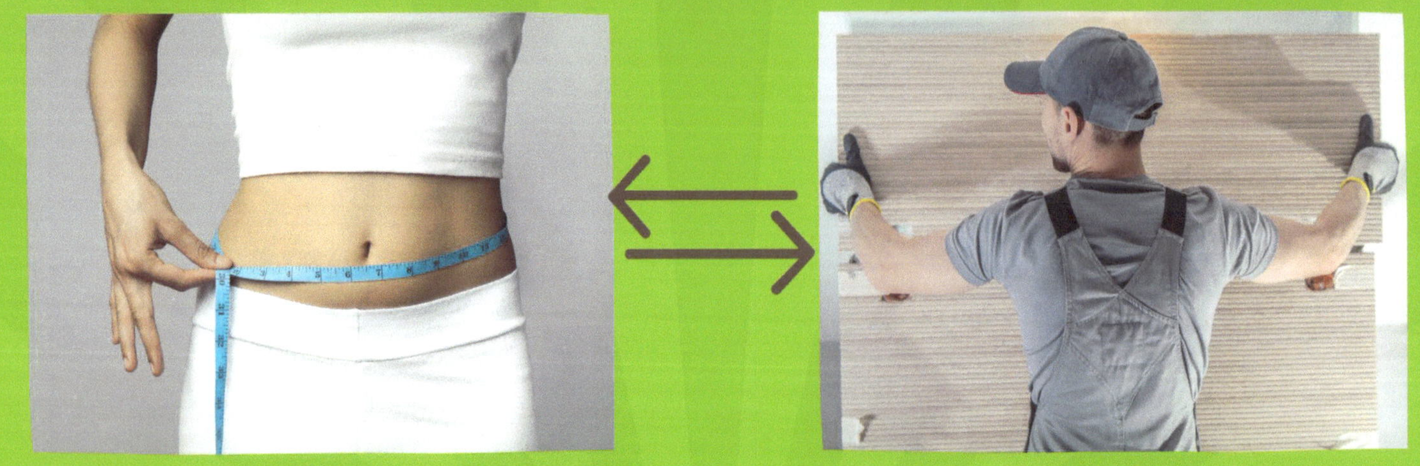

thin

sottile

large

largo

easy

facile

difficult

difficile

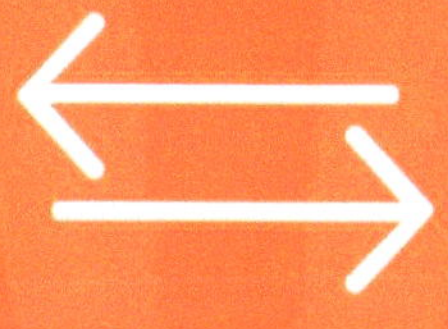

stand up

alzarsi

sit down

sedersi

sweet

dolce

salty

salato

heavy

pesante

light

leggero

in

dentro

out

fuori

dirty

sporco

clean

pulito

close

chiudere

open

aprire

pencils

matite

clock

orologio

key

chiave

book

libro

bed

letto

crib

culla

table

tavolo

chair

sedia

car

automobile

bike

bicicletta

plane

aereo

boat

barca

train

treno

helicopter

elicottero

firetruck

camion dei pompieri

firefighter

pompiere

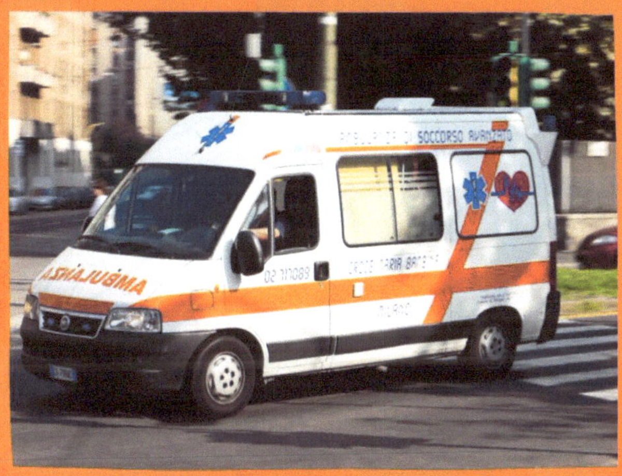

ambulance

ambulanza

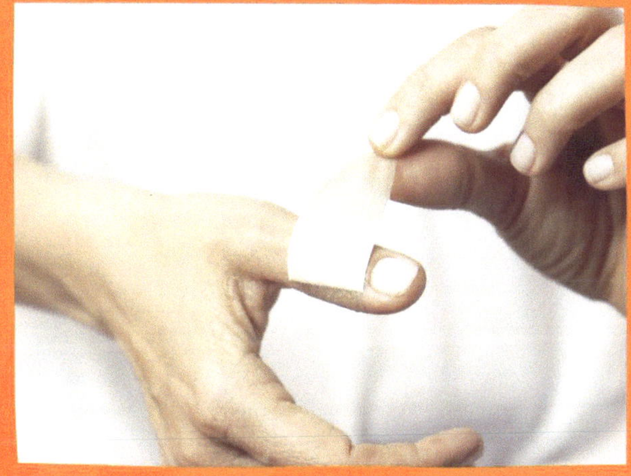

bandage

benda

paramedic

paramedico

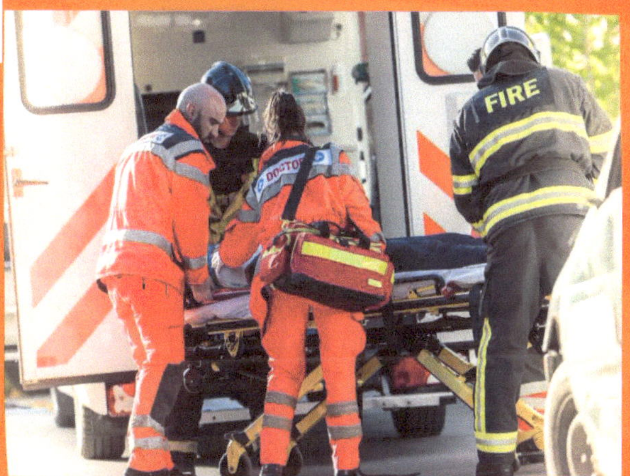

rescue team

squadra di soccorso

forest

foresta

mountain

montagna

grass

erba

sand

sabbia

tree

albero

flower

fiore

butterfly

farfalla

ant

formica

cat

gatto

dog

cane

horse

cavallo

mouse

topo

cow

mucca

pig

maiale

sheep

pecora

duck

anatra

goose

oca

rabbit

coniglio

fish

pesce

vet

veterinario

doctor

dottore

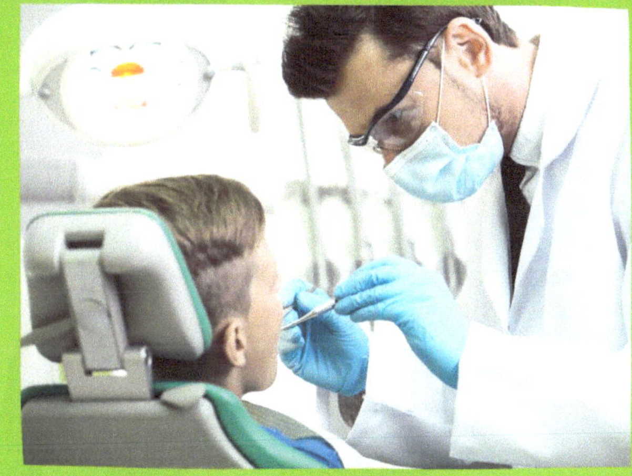

dentist

dentista

pharmacist

farmacista

nurse

infermiere

head

testa

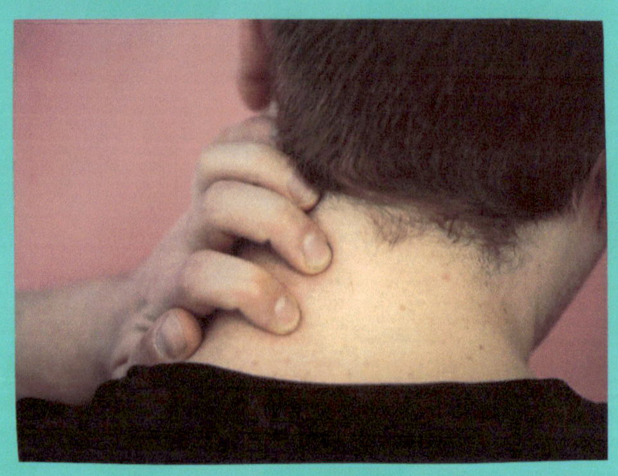

neck

collo

foot

piede

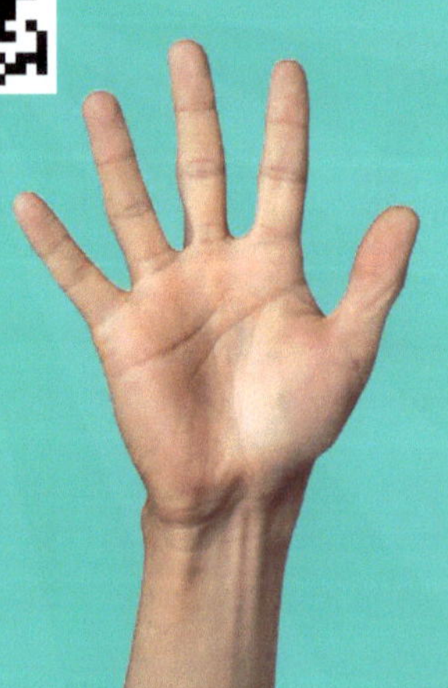

hand

mano

teeth

denti

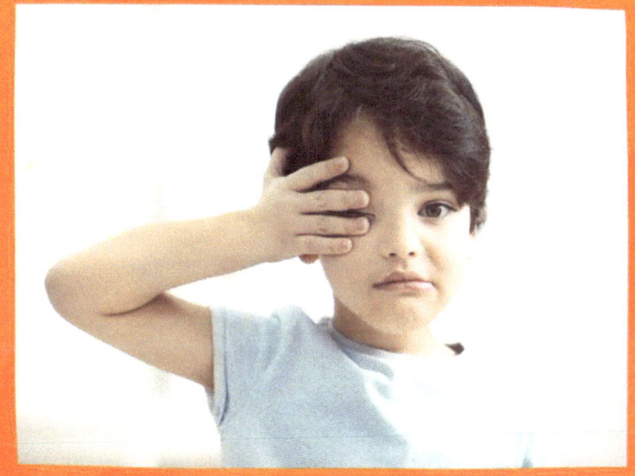

eye

occhio

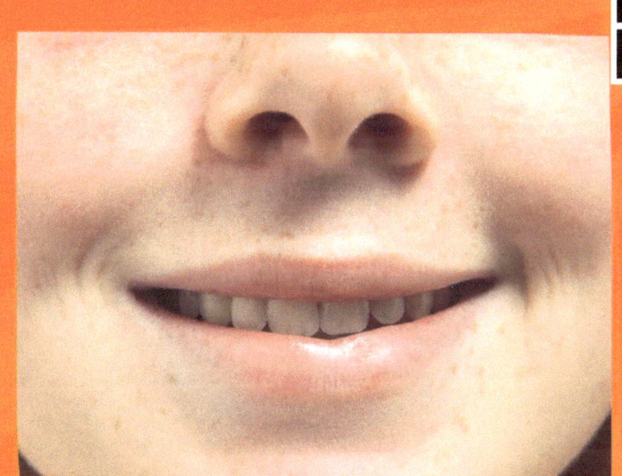

mouth

bocca

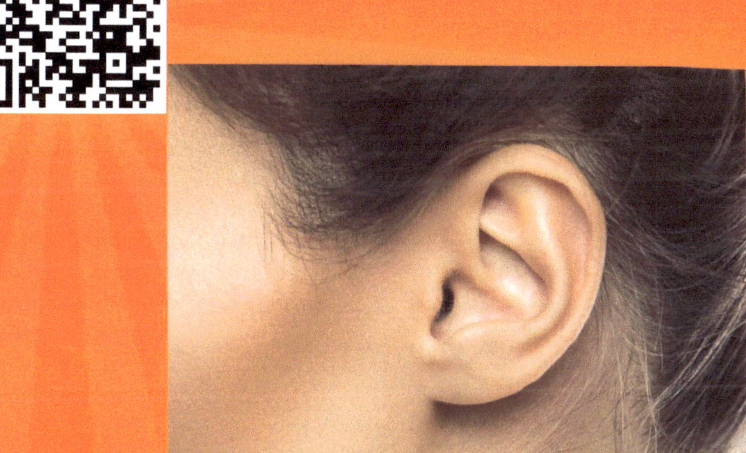

ear

orecchio

hat

cappello

dress

vestito

pants

pantaloni

shoes

scarpe

coat

cappotto

scarf

sciarpa

umbrella

ombrello

glasses

occhiali

sun

sole

cloudy

nuvoloso

rainy

piovoso

moon

luna